Knowing Your Limits: Setting Healthy Boundaries to Take Charge of Your Life

TABLE OF CONTENT

Introduction

Life can occasionally resemble a never-ending roster of tasks. Between work, family, friends, and community obligations, there never seems to be enough time to get it all done. And with the always-connected nature of modern life, it's easier than ever before to end up overcommitted, overwhelmed, and stretched too thin.

If this sounds familiar, you're not alone. In our people-pleasing quest to be helpful, liked, and seen as "good," many of us take on too much. We say yes when we really want to say no out of guilt, anxiety about letting others down, or a lack of self-confidence in our own needs and priorities. The result? Our health, happiness, and relationships suffer.

Healthy boundaries are the antidote. They are the lines we draw around ourselves to protect our time, energy, and sense of self. Boundaries give us the space we need to care for ourselves first before pouring from an empty cup. And contrary to what some may believe, boundaries also allow us to deepen our connections. Research shows that relationships built on mutual respect, trust, and autonomy are more fulfilling and lasting.

So, why do so many of us find it difficult with setting boundaries? Old habits die hard. Many of us were raised to put others first, sacrifice our needs for the "greater good," and never utter the word "no." We confuse selflessness with people-pleasing, giving in with being "nice." And when we do try to set a boundary, we are met with resistance or guilting. Family members accuse us of being selfish, friends get upset that we can't do favors anymore, and coworkers resent our newfound work-life balance.

But making a change is possible with self-awareness, practice, and commitment to prioritizing our health and well-being. By learning our limits, honoring our feelings, and communicating kindly but firmly, we can reset unhealthy dynamics. The road won't always be smooth, but the effort is well worth it.

This book provides strategies to take back your time, energy, and power. You'll learn how to:

- Identify your core values and priorities
- Recognize when to say no without guilt or apology
- Establish healthy boundaries with family, at work, and in relationships
- Protect your schedule from overcommitment and constant busyness
- Detach from toxic relationships and dynamics
- Communicate your needs clearly and with compassion
- Overcome anxiety about disappointing others
- Respond to resistance, guilting, and manipulation
- Stick to your boundaries while still being loving

- And much more

Life is filled with demands and obligations outside of our control. But we consistently possess the ability to choose our response. This book will give you the tools to stop being defined by others' expectations and finally live life on your own terms.

I'll share plenty of relatable anecdotes from my own journey learning to set better boundaries. We'll also hear from psychologists, counselors, and people who have successfully transformed their relationships through the power of boundaries. While establishing healthy boundaries takes practice, self-awareness, and shaking off old habits, the benefits make it well worth it.

So, if you're tired of constant stress, exhaustion, resentment, and saying yes when you really mean no, the guidance in this book can help you regain balance and take charge of your life. Let's begin the journey toward self-care, fulfillment, and deeper connections!

Chapter 1: Understanding Boundaries and Why They Matter

Life can easily turn into an endless cascade of responsibilities and demands on our time. Work projects pile up, friends ask for favors, and family needs support. Add in our own interests and hobbies, and there just never seems to be enough hours in the day to get it all done.

Many of us cope by endlessly saying yes and pushing ourselves to the brink of burnout. We operate under the flawed belief that self-sacrifice is noble and utterly neglect our own needs. Sure, it can feel good at first to please others and be the helpful, generous person. But without healthy boundaries, we end up depleted, resentful, and struggling to stay afloat.

This chapter provides essential background for why boundaries matter so much for a balanced, joyful life. We'll explore:

- What boundaries actually are
- Indications that you should improve your boundary-setting
- The risks of being overly compliant and not saying no
- How a lack of boundaries affects your self-esteem and mental health
- Why boundaries foster better relationships
- How to prepare mentally to start setting boundaries

Let's dive in and start learning how to take back control of your time, energy, and life!

What Are Boundaries And What's Their Significance?

- Boundaries are the physical, emotional, mental, and digital lines we draw around ourselves to distinguish what is our responsibility vs. someone else's

- Having clear boundaries allows us to protect our time for self-care, rest, and the activities that nourish us

- Boundaries also help us maintain a sense of self separate from others and know our own needs and dealbreakers

- Mentally healthy boundaries are flexible when needed but still firmly upheld most of the time

Put simply, boundaries are our defined limits and rules for what we find acceptable and unacceptable in our lives. Boundaries can apply to our interactions, responsibilities, emotional availability, values, time, physical space, digital presence, finances, sexual intimacy, spiritual beliefs, and more.

Having clear boundaries is essential for a peaceful, balanced life. Without them, we end up overcommitted, overwhelmed, drained, and stretched too thin. Our well-being, both physically and mentally, is negatively impacted, along with our emotional health

Strong boundaries allow us to:

- Protect our time for self-care, rest, and personal interests

- Reduce stress by not taking on too many responsibilities

- Preserve our energy so we don't end up exhausted and burnt out

- Uphold our values so we don't compromise our ethics or do
  things we regret

- Maintain a sense of self separate from others and the
  demands placed on us

- Know our own needs, priorities, and dealbreakers so we can
  express them

- Regain control over areas of our life feeling chaotic or
  neglected

Boundaries may feel restrictive at first, but they actually grant us freedom. Freedom from constant overwhelm, resentment, guilt, and the uneasy feeling of being spread too thin. The next time you are tempted to say yes to something that takes you away from rest, hobbies, or self-care, remember that boundaries exist to protect what you cherish most.

Indications that you should improve your boundary-setting

Most of us need stronger boundaries in certain areas of our lives. The following symptoms may indicate it's time to reevaluate your limits:

- You frequently feel stressed, irritated, resentful,
  overwhelmed, or exhausted

- You struggle to find time for basic self-care like sleep,
  healthy food, exercise

- You often say yes when you really want to say no out of guilt or obligation
- You take on favors and tasks beyond your capacity just to please others
- You feel constantly behind, always playing catch up, never getting a break
- You have trouble fully relaxing on vacations and time off
- Anxiety, dread, or anger arises when you think about certain relationships or commitments
- You struggle with codependency in relationships and lack a sense of self
- You compromise your values or ethics to avoid confrontation or disappointment

Pay attention if any of these resonate strongly. Your mind and body are attempting to communicate an important message. Don't ignore the signs of poor boundaries for too long. The costs to your mental and physical health are simply too great.

On the other hand, a life with healthy boundaries looks like:

- Time and energy for self-care, hobbies, passions, and rest
- Low stress and a sense of calm and ease each day
- Clarity around your own needs, wants, values and priorities
- The ability to say no without guilt or over-explaining yourself
- Mutually fulfilling relationships built on respect

- A strong sense of self separate from your responsibilities and roles
- The freedom to relax fully during your downtime

The more control we regain over our time, energy, space, information intake, emotional availability and priorities, the more freedom and peace we can experience. So let's explore how to start building those much-needed boundaries!

The Risks of Being Overly Compliant and Not Saying No

Many of us, especially women, are socialized from an early age to be compliant and acquiescent. Girls are often taught to be polite, quiet, and people-pleasing so as not to inconvenience others. In the words of Margaret Atwood, "A man stands firmly on the earth, while a woman is expected to remain on a pedestal."

So, we minimize our own needs, avoid making direct asks, speak indirectly, fill uncomfortable silences, and end up saying yes even when we want to say no. This breeds resentment, anxiety, lack of trust in ourselves, and physical and emotional exhaustion over time. Here are just some of the risks of not establishing healthy boundaries:

Loss of Self

When we don't listen to our inner voice and internal wisdom, it becomes muted. We can lose touch with our own interests, values, passions, personalities, and identities. Without boundaries, there is nothing to distinguish our sense of self and rhythms from those around us. We exist for others but forget who we are in the process.

Caregiver Burnout

Women especially fall into the trap of constantly caring for others at the expense of themselves. Whether it be children, partners, parents, friends, or co-workers, our society conditions women to be nurturing helpers first and foremost. However, it's impossible for anyone to give when their own cup is empty. Self-care has to come first.

Resentment and Bitterness

Saying yes when we really want to say no breeds resentment, anger, and bitterness over time. We may blame others for taking advantage of our time and energy. But boundaries exist precisely so we can take responsibility for our choices and limit how much we give away.

Anxiety from Overcommitment

Agreeing to more than we can handle leads to a constant state of anxiety, pressure, and feeling overwhelmed. Our to-do list grows, time anxiety sets in, and simple tasks start inducing panic. Life feels frustratingly out of control.

Lack of Trust and Honesty in Relationships

If we don't express our true needs and feelings, resentment festers.

Honesty and intimacy suffers. No one can ever fully relax and trust someone without boundaries. Expressing our authentic thoughts and emotions cultivates deeper connections.

Emotional and Physical Exhaustion

When we don't budget our limited time and energy, we eventually hit empty. Running on fumes leads to emotional numbness, depression, and physical illness. Our minds and bodies demand we slow down but we fail to listen.

Difficulty Relaxing and Enjoying Downtime

If we don't protect our time intentionally, others will commandeer it. Without boundaries, we devalue our own right to rest and enjoy leisure time. But downtime is essential, not a guilty luxury. It is the space where creativity and inspiration is renewed.

How a Lack of Boundaries Affects Your Self-Esteem and Mental Health

Failing to set loving limits and boundaries for how you allow people to treat you reflects a lack of self-care, self-compassion, and self-respect. You may tell yourself it's "selfless" to do anything for anyone who asks. But being endlessly compliant, readily available, and unable to say no is rooted in lack of self-worth and fear of disappointing others or being disliked.

Having weak boundaries signals to others they can treat you poorly or take advantage without consequence. You teach people that your time and needs aren't all that important or worth considering. This gradually undermines your self-confidence and self-esteem.

Your mental health will inevitably suffer without strong boundaries. Here are a few of the usual outcomes:

- **Chronic stress** - The unrelenting demands and pressures leads to elevated cortisol and adrenaline. Over time, chronic stress causes anxiety, depression, burnout, and even post-traumatic stress like symptoms in severe cases.

- **Exhaustion and emotional numbness** - When we deplete our energy reserves, we stop feeling much at all. Anxious worries get replaced by deadened numbness. We run on auto-pilot just to survive the days.

- **Resentment and anger** - Suppressed resentment that we bury so as not to seem ungrateful or selfish inevitably bubbles up. We may even resent loved ones and friends because of their demands.

- **Poor self-esteem and lack of self-worth** - When we don't honor our needs and time, we signal to ourselves and others we aren't worthy of care and respect. This slowly diminishes our sense of value.

- **Loss of passion, interests, creativity** - When our lives revolve around obligations, we lose touch with what brings us joy. Over time, our passions and creativity fade without nourishment.

- **Addiction risk** - Lack of boundaries and depleted dopamine reserves make us vulnerable to addictions and substance abuse as a way to cope.

Make no mistake - bad boundaries are hazardous to your health and sense of self. But the good news is, even small steps to start creating healthy boundaries can dramatically improve your mental well-being and relationships.

Why Boundaries Foster Better Relationships

Boundaries are not meant to push people away or create distance, although that may occasionally happen. Rather, boundaries allow intimacy and closeness to deepen in healthy, mutually fulfilling ways.

Research shows that relationships built on mutual personal autonomy, respect, and freedom have the greatest satisfaction. Control and coercion breed resentment. Here are some ways strong boundaries improve connections:

- **They create trust** - When people know where they stand with you, trust builds. No one has to second guess or walk on eggshells.
- **They set standards** - Boundaries communicate the kind of treatment you expect from others. You teach people how you wish to be respected.

- **They allow honesty** - With limits in place, you can be truthful about feelings and needs without fear. Truth strengthens closeness.

- **They generate gratitude** - When you conserve your time and energy, you feel gratitude for those who respect your limits. You cherish time together more.

- **They prevent resentment** -Voicing your authentic needs rather than silently keeping score prevents later bitterness and explosion.

- **They earn you respect** - You gain self-respect by honoring your needs. And you earn respect from others by upholding healthy limits.

- **They allow relaxation** - With boundaries, you can fully relax into downtime knowing you took care of your responsibilities already. No need for guilt.

In short, boundaries create the space for freedom. And within this freedom, intimacy and connection can deepen. Keep this in mind during difficult conversations or when others challenge your limits. Boundaries ultimately nurture relationships rooted in mutual care, trust, respect, and responsibility.

How to Prepare Yourself Mentally to Start Setting Boundaries

Learning to set boundaries after a lifetime of being overly compliant takes practice. You've likely internalized some unhelpful beliefs like:

- Saying no is selfish
- Going with the flow is being easygoing
- Taking on a lot shows you're capable
- Wanting time to yourself is indulgent
- Speaking up makes you "difficult"
- Disappointing people means you're uncaring

Transforming these thought patterns is half the battle. Here are some tips:

- **Gain clarity about your values** - Identify what holds true importance for you. Make a list of your top values and what aligns with your best self. Let these guide and motivate you.
- **Identify past resentment** - Make note of situations that made you feel resentful, taken advantage of, stressed or unhappy. You don't want repeats.
- **Learn your limits** - What circumstances, behaviors or demands make you uncomfortable? Knowing your limits ahead of time makes communicating them easier.
- **Practice saying no** - Roleplay scenarios in low-risk settings to build up your assertiveness muscle and reduce future anxiety.

- **Start small** - Don't overhaul everything overnight. Make incremental changes so you don't get overwhelmed. Small steps add up.

- **Know it gets easier** - The awkwardness and discomfort when setting boundaries lessens quickly with practice and experience.

- **Find supportive friends** - Seek encouraging friends who will cheer you on as you get more vocal about your needs. Avoid naysayers early on.

- **Learn to tolerate discomfort** - Standing up for yourself may not always feel good in the moment. But you'll respect yourself, and you deserve that.

- **Focus on freedom** - Remind yourself that boundaries free up energy and time for self-care and the activities you cherish most. They limit stress and overwhelm.

- **Be kind but firm** - Boundaries aren't about aggression or punishment. Communicate your limits with compassion while also being direct and consistent.

- **Trust your gut** - Listen to your instincts and inner voice. If something feels wrong deep down or crosses your values, don't doubt yourself just to avoid conflict.

With the right mindset and preparation, you'll be ready to start defining the healthy boundaries that will improve your life immensely. Let's now move on to explore how to identify your specific needs.

Chapter 2: Knowing Your Needs and Where to Draw the Line

In the last chapter, we explored why boundaries are so critical for a balanced life. Now let's get practical. Defining your personal boundaries starts with getting to know your needs, priorities, values and limits.

This self-knowledge provides the foundation to then communicate your boundaries kindly but firmly to others. When you are clear within yourself first, expressing your boundaries outwardly becomes much easier.

Here's what we'll cover in this chapter:

- Clarifying your core values
- Assessing your natural rhythms and personality traits
- Identifying your must-have priorities
- Determining your dealbreakers
- Knowing your limitations
- Understanding your emotional bandwidth
- Practicing self-awareness and listening inward
- Exercises to discover your boundaries
- Finding your voice and building confidence

Let's get started unraveling what really matters most to you!

Clarifying Your Core Values

Values are your deeply held beliefs about what is important, desirable and aligns with your best self. They serve as guiding principles for your choices and behavior.

When you know your values clearly, decisions become much simpler. You rely less on outside opinions and validation. You become motivated from within to uphold your values with boundaries.

Common personal values include:

- Authenticity
- Achievement
- Adventure
- Autonomy
- Compassion
- Contribution
- Creativity
- Community
- Ethical living
- Family
- Financial freedom
- Flexibility
- Gratitude
- Growth
- Happiness
- Health

- Honesty
- Humor
- Independence
- Intimacy
- Justice
- Kindness
- Knowledge
- Leadership
- Learning
- Love
- Loyalty
- Meaning
- Openness
- Order
- Peace
- Pleasure
- Purpose
- Reliability
- Respect
- Responsibility
- Security
- Self-development
- Spirituality
- Stability
- Success

- Trustworthiness
- Wisdom

Take time to reflect on which values light you up and align with your best self. Make a list of your top 5-10 core values. Post them somewhere visible to guide your choices and priorities. Let these values motivate you to set needed boundaries.

Assessing Your Natural Rhythms and Personality Traits

We each have natural rhythms, habits and personality traits that impact how we need to structure our days and environment. Take inventory of yours:

- Do you tend to be more active in the morning or late at night?
- Do you prefer lots of variety or consistency in your routine?
- What types of environments help you recharge - quiet, social, active, calm?
- Are you more introverted or extroverted?
- Do you prefer planning ahead or improvising?
- How much alone time do you need?
- How do you handle stress best - with movement, quiet, connection, rest?

Start recording when your energy levels dip during the day. Pay attention to your innate preferences rather than powering through. This self-understanding allows you to set boundaries aligned with your personality - like blocking out alone time and planning active socializing when you have the most energy.

Your boundaries will be personalized to honor your natural rhythms and tendencies. For example, if crowds drain you, limit volunteer events to once a month. If you think best in the mornings, schedule creative work first before tackling administrative tasks. Stop forcing yourself into rigid expectations of what you "should" like or endure. Your needs are allowed to be unique. Listen and you'll discover how to create a life that honors your natural self.

Identifying Your Must-Have Priorities

What activities bring you joy, energy and meaning? Make a list of your must-have priorities - the things that make life rich and fulfilling for you.

For example, your priorities might include:

- Creative hobbies like writing, art, music

- Time in nature or exercising outdoors

- Nurturing your spirituality through practices like prayer or meditation

- Regular date nights or quality time with your partner

- Making home-cooked meals and enjoying them slowly

- Spending time playing with your kids

- Maintaining close friendships through weekly catch-up calls

- Lifelong learning by taking interesting classes

Rank your priorities by importance. Schedule time for your top priorities before anything else. Protect them with boundaries by learning to say no to requests that interfere.

Be honest with yourself about things you value but have let fall by the wayside due to lack of boundaries. For example, maybe you've wanted to join a community choir or take an Italian cooking class for years but haven't made the time. Align your actions with your intentions.

Determining Your Dealbreakers

Your dealbreakers are behaviors or circumstances that you find intolerable and unacceptable for your life. Knowing these ahead of time makes it easier to set firm boundaries when needed.

For example, common dealbreakers include:

- Abuse or violence of any kind
- Addiction or substance abuse
- Chronic dishonesty
- Severe disrespect of boundaries
- Unsafe behavior that puts you or loved ones in danger
- Unethical or illegal activity
- Severe dysfunction that is unlikely to change
- Repeated infidelity or betrayal of trust

Make a list of your dealbreakers. While we all have weaknesses and room for growth, decide what would be grounds for ending a relationship or walking away from a situation to protect your well-being.

Trust yourself. If something feels deeply wrong or threatening, it likely is. Don't doubt your inner wisdom just because someone else tells you to "lighten up" or tolerate bad behavior. Boundaries keep you safe.

Knowing Your Limitations

Life asks much of us - perhaps more than is reasonable or healthy in our hustle-focused culture. To prevent burnout and depletion, you must know your limitations and honor them.

Consider limitations like:

- How many social engagements you can handle per week before feeling drained?
- The number of work hours that are productive and sustainable for you
- How many family obligations you can manage alongside other priorities?
- How often you can assist others before needing to take a break?
- How much noise and chaos you can tolerate before needing quiet?
- How much alone time you require to recharge fully?

Tune in to when you start feeling overwhelmed, irritated, or exhausted. Those are clues you may be pushing past healthy limits. Pull back and reassess.

For example, if more than 10 hours of social time per week leaves you wiped out, set that as a boundary. If you get impatient and snippy after 3 consecutive workdays, build in comp days for yourself.

Give yourself permission to know and honor your natural limits without judgment. You don't need to measure up to anyone else's capacity. Do what feels healthy and right for you.

Understanding Your Emotional Bandwidth

In addition to physical and mental limits, accept that you have a finite amount of emotional energy to give. When bandwidth gets maxed out, it's time to temporarily limit your emotional availability.

For instance, while you may love supporting friends and lending an empathetic ear, make sure you take breaks when you start feeling:

- Impatient or short with others
- Resentful of their needs
- Drained by vent sessions
- Preoccupied with your own worries
- Unable to focus fully

Tune in to your levels of patience, joy, enthusiasm, and compassion.

Pull back when your emotional reserves run low. Suggest alternatives like taking a walk rather than sitting and venting for hours.

Protecting your emotional bandwidth also means setting limits on:

- News intake if stories create anxiety or sadness
- Toxic people who leave you feeling bad about yourself
- Manipulators who guilt you into more than you want to give
- Drama and constant complaining without solutions

Preserve your emotional energy for the people and activities that bring you joy and meaning. Learn to let the rest go.

Practicing Self-Awareness and Listening Inward

Noticing your needs, rhythms, values, and limits requires regular self-reflection. Make time to check in with yourself, especially during major transitions or times of increased demand. Self-awareness practices might include:

- Keeping a journal to process feelings and recent experiences
- Daily meditation or breathing exercises
- Reflecting on what's working well or feeling off-balance
- Connecting with your intuitive insights and inner knowledge.
- Spending time in nature to gain clarity
- Discussing challenges with a trusted friend or therapist
- Identifying lessons learned from hardships or conflicts

Make sure to listen to your body's signals as well. Physical symptoms like fatigue, stomach troubles, headaches, and muscle tightness often reflect overwhelmed boundaries. Do not disregard the messages your body is attempting to convey.

Make self-check-ins a regular habit, not just a crisis response. Be proactive about knowing your evolving needs and limits over the years. Change is inevitable; make sure your boundaries adapt accordingly.

Exercises to Discover Your Boundaries

Here are some helpful exercises to gain more clarity:

Review Your Calendar

Analyze how you currently spend your time. What feels depleting vs. energizing? What commitments could be dropped, delegated, or minimized? Where do you need to make more space for self-care and priorities?

Vision Your Ideal Day

Imagine a day where you felt balanced, energized, and fully yourself. What does this day look like? What boundaries would be in place? Use this vision to identify gaps between your real and ideal life.

Write Your Own Obituary

Envision your life story when you're gone. What do you want people to remember? What contributions, accomplishments, and relationships matter most to you? Use this perspective to define your core priorities now.

Identify Your Temptation Triggers

When are you most likely to cave on your boundaries? When you're tired? Feeling guilty? Lonely? By knowing your weaknesses, you can prepare your responses in advance or avoid those situations entirely.

Make a No List

What do you commit to that leaves you feeling resentful or obligated? Make a list of things you do for others but not yourself. Start eliminating or delegating these.

Define Your Rules of Engagement

What are your rules of engagement for different domains - like work hours, family visits, helping favors, etc? Outline the boundaries that would make you feel happiest and in control.

Role-Play Responses

Practice saying no and setting limits in low-stakes situations with friends. The more you build this muscle, the easier it becomes. Use mantras like "Let me check my schedule first" to give yourself time.

Keep returning to these exercises periodically to check in with yourself. Your needs will change over time. Update your boundaries accordingly.

Finding Your Voice and Building Confidence

After years of being overly compliant and not voicing your needs, the thought of setting boundaries likely stirs up some self-doubt and anxiety. That's very normal.

Here are some tips to build confidence in setting boundaries:

- **Start small** - Begin with low-stakes requests from acquaintances or strangers first. Say no to handing out flyers or street petitions before declining favors from loved ones. Build up slowly.

- **Practice privately first** - Role-play boundary setting alone or with a coach. Having words ready that feel authentic to you makes communicating easier.

- **Know your worth** - Remind yourself that protecting your time and energy shows self-respect. You matter.

- **Tolerate discomfort** - The awkwardness or confrontation of setting a boundary feels uncomfortable. But it's temporary. Stay strong knowing it gets easier.

- **Pause before responding** - When asked for a favor, buy yourself time to consider. Say you'll check your schedule and get back to them. Don't feel pressured to answer immediately.

- **Reflect on your past resentment** - Remember times you've felt taken advantage of. Don't let those patterns repeat. You have permission to set limits now.

- **Have a mantra** - Come up with a phrase that helps you stand firm like "My health is my top priority right now." Repeat it when doubting yourself.

- **Focus on the long term** - Keep the vision of your happier life with boundaries front and center. Short term discomfort leads to long term fulfillment.

- **Celebrate wins** - Reward yourself each time you successfully uphold a boundary. Positive reinforcement builds self-trust and motivation.

- **Find supportive friends** - Surround yourself with people who applaud your growth. Their belief in you bolsters confidence.

Trust that setting boundaries gets less intimidating with practice. Keep strengthening your self-awareness, listening to your needs, defining your limits, and communicating them with compassion. You've got this!

Chapter 3: Setting Boundaries with Family

The home front is often where boundary issues first emerge. The deep intimacy and history of family relationships can make setting limits feel complicated. Parents, siblings, and extended family may struggle to see you as an autonomous adult. Additionally, family patterns and roles solidify over years to the point they feel immutable. Taking on new boundaries challenges the status quo. Some may resist the changes and loss of control.

But transforming family dynamics is possible with courage, communication, and consistency. You may need to disrupt unhealthy patterns and become the catalyst for growth. It won't always be comfortable. But standing firm in your experience and needs is the only path to a more balanced and mutually supportive family environment.

This chapter provides guidance on:

- Setting boundaries with parents
- Balancing closeness and independence with siblings
- Saying no to family events or requests that cross your boundaries
- Managing extended family dynamics and obligations
- Communicating needs kindly but directly
- Responding when boundaries are challenged or disrespected
- Rebuilding broken trust and resentments
- Strategies for detaching from family dysfunction
- Maintaining boundaries while still being loving

Let's explore how to cultivate healthy family relationships based on mutual respect.

Setting Boundaries with Parents

The parent-child relationship is filled with innate complexities. Parents often struggle to let go of authority and decision-making power over their children, even into adulthood. Additionally, entrenched childhood roles and dynamics persist, requiring conscious work to dismantle and redefine.

Here are some tips for setting boundaries with parents:

- **Communicate directly** - Don't hint or expect them to intuit your needs. Respectfully discuss the specific changes you hope to see.

- **Don't wait for permission** - You're an adult now. Kindly inform them of your decisions rather than asking for approval.

- **Limit information overload** - Be selective about what you share to avoid unsolicited feedback about your choices. Keep some details private.

- **Manage expectations** - If they expect constant contact, clarify how often you're able to call or visit. Stick to defined windows.

- **Limit advice** - Don't automatically turn to your parents for guidance now. Seek counsel from unbiased friends or a therapist instead when needed.

- **Establish visitor rules** - If your parents stay with you, define clear guest protocols about privacy, meals, quiet hours, duties, etc so you don't end up feeling like a child again.

- **Meet in neutral locations** - When possible, see them outside the home environment where old dynamics get triggered. Meet at a restaurant for dinner instead.

- **Take a timeout when needed** - If tensions escalate, call a break in the conversation. Revisit when emotions have calmed down.

- **Seek professional help** - If boundary issues lead to ongoing conflicts, enlist a therapist to mediate productive conversations. An objective third party can uncover dysfunctional patterns that you may be too close to see.

Be patient with the process. It took years to build the parent-child paradigm, and it will take time to reshape it. But staying rooted in mutual love, respect and maturity will reconstruct your relationship on healthier ground.

Balancing Closeness and Independence with Siblings

Siblings often become our closest comrades thanks to all the shared history, laughter, and fights (!) throughout childhood. We confide in and seek advice from siblings on matters we may not tell anyone else.

But too much closeness as adults, especially if you live in the same city, risks perpetuating childhood roles and limiting full individual growth. Here are some tips to balance connection and boundaries:

- **Limit vent sessions** - Be cautious of getting involved as a sounding board for every concern or disagreement with parents, kids, or partners. Redirect them to seek support from friends or a counselor when needed.

- **Say no to comparisons** - If a sibling tries to compare career milestones, parenting approaches, etc gently but firmly tell them you're each on your own path.

- **Establish visit protocols** - Agree on expectations before extended visits about length of stay, expenses, activities, alone time needed, discipline of kids, emergency contingency plans, etc so unspoken resentments don't build.

- **Limit unsolicited advice** - While some input can be helpful, make it clear when and on what topics you want guidance. On other matters, simply listen without commentary.

- **Discuss finances separately** - To avoid tensions, have a boundary that money matters like loans, gifts, inheritances, etc are private and not up for judgement between siblings.

- **Take space when needed** - If siblings become overly involved, intrusive, or draining, put more space between visits, calls, texts. Politely explain you just need breathing room.

- **Focus on the present** - Let go of the rosy past or slights from childhood. Show up fully for each other in the age and stage you're in now.

Remember that creating healthy space between siblings does not diminish the love; it strengthens it through respect for each other as individuals. Distance allows you both to fully show up.

Saying No to Family Events or Requests That Cross Your Boundaries

Holidays, family vacations, weddings, rituals - there's no shortage of obligatory gatherings. But not every occasion may feel like a celebration to you, especially if family dynamics are strained.

It's okay to say no to requests or events that compromise your values, priorities, or wellbeing - even if that displeases others. Polite decline is better than showing up with resentment.

Here are suggestions for skipping events or setting attendance boundaries:

- **Send regrets, not excuses** - Decline politely without feeling a need to excessively explain yourself. " I regret that I won't be able to attend this year, but I wish you a wonderful holiday."

- **Propose an alternative** - Offer to celebrate together in a different way, like an intimate dinner vs. a large crowed event. This shows you still care.

- **Delegate a representative** - If an important milestone like a graduation or wedding, send your partner or a friend in your place when you need to decline. Have them convey your well wishes.

- **Skip the drama-filled events** - Be selective about events certain family members will attend who affect you negatively. Don't feel obligated. Protect your peace.

- **Set time limits ahead of time** - If anxious about a gathering, commit to just a set number of hours. Honoring your limit prevents building resentment.

- **Bookend with self-care** - Plan something nurturing before and after an obligation to recover and reset. A massage, hike or bubble bath can help you show up and decompress.

- **Request accommodations** - If crowds or noise are an issue, ask to celebrate in a smaller subgroup or alternate location. Many will happily accommodate.

At the end of the day, you know what's best for your mental health. Listen to your instincts. Declining an invitation is appropriate when the costs to your wellbeing outweigh the benefits. Just be selectively honest - no need to dredge up every past grievance! State your choice simply and without judgment.

Managing Extended Family Dynamics and Obligations

Cousins, aunts, uncles, grandparents - our extended families often have as much influence over our early lives as our parents and siblings. But as adults, those once close bonds can fade.

Still, a sense of family obligation persists. Here are tips to balance connection and boundaries with extended relatives:

- **Let go of guilt** - Don't get down on yourself for losing touch. It's normal as lives expand. Do what you can when possible.

- **Check in occasionally** - Send a text, forward a news article, or mail a holiday card to maintain threads without huge investment. They'll appreciate the thought.

- **Define your role** - Decide if you want to be a leader bringing the family together or prefer just showing up. Neither is right or wrong.

- **Limit gossip** - Be careful not to get embroiled in family gossip. Redirect conversations to positive topics about their lives and interests.

- **Avoid falling into old dynamics** - Visit extended family independently rather than with relatives you have unresolved issues with. Limit what old stories get triggered.

- **Keep visits short and sweet** - Prioritize quality over quantity time. It's better to leave wanting more than overstaying your welcome.

- **Contribute your skills** - Offer what comes naturally - maybe organizing get-togethers, documenting family history through photos, or creating memory books.

- **Set a budget** - To avoid financial stresses, define what you can reasonably afford for gifts or travel to distant family. Don't overextend yourself.

- **Take space when needed** - If extended family becomes invasive, meddling, or demanding, politely decline invitations for a period of time. Focus inward.

While extended family brings richness to our lives, don't neglect your nuclear family and friends. Prioritize those closest rather than over-rotating energy trying to maintain a wide web of kin.

Communicating Needs Kindly But Directly

Some family members will readily accept your evolving boundaries. Others may need help understanding the changes. Have compassion. Avoid announcing boundaries abruptly without context. Here are tips for effectively communicating your needs:

- **Plan the conversation** - Write talking points in advance so you're calm and focused, not reactive. Have realistic outcomes defined.

- **Pick a neutral time and place** - Don't start boundary talks on holidays when emotions run high. Have the discussion privately once things have settled.

- **Use plenty of "I" statements** - Use "I need, I feel, I want" etc rather than accusatory "you" statements. Take ownership of your experience.

- **Be specific** - Rather than vague grievances, offer concrete examples of what you need moving forward - like limited advice giving, more notice before visits, enforced quiet hours, etc.

- **Express appreciation** - Start the conversation by expressing how much you value their importance in your life. This softens defensiveness.

- **Seek to understand their side** - Ask why they respond the way they do or feel hurt by your boundaries. Seek common ground.

- **Make requests, not demands** - A demanding tone will shut down dialogue fast. Frame your boundaries as polite requests.

- **Give it time to sink in** - Your family may need time to process changes to your relationship. Allow a few days before a follow up call.

- **Compromise where possible** - If a need isn't non-negotiable, offer flexibility in your request. Collaboration fosters commitment.

- **Reinforce in action** - Uphold your stated boundaries consistently in your behavior over time. Consistency builds new habits.

With time and genuine listening on both sides, you can rebuild family relationships on a foundation of mutual understanding and respect for your needs as an adult.

Responding When Boundaries Are Challenged or Disrespected

Despite your best efforts, some family members will push back on healthy boundaries. Resistance is likely rooted in fear - of losing control, being abandoned, or growing apart.

Here are techniques for responding firmly yet lovingly:

- **Remain calm** - If they get reactive, take some deep breaths. Don't counter aggression with aggression. Stay grounded in your truth.

- **Recognize their emotions** - "I understand that this is distressing. Let's give it some time and revisit this when we've both had space to process."

- **Rephrase your boundary clearly** - Repeat in a neutral tone what is and isn't working for you. Don't get pulled into debate.

- **Stand your ground** - Respect their perspective but don't cave just to keep the peace. Compromising your needs won't lead to lasting harmony.

- **Give reassurance** - Affirm your unconditional love. For parents, emphasize you are still their child even as you create new boundaries appropriate for adulthood.

- **Suggest counseling** - If communication breaks down, propose seeing a family therapist together. Having a mediator creates needed structure and neutrality.

- **Give it space** - Once you've made your position clear, step back. Let them sit with it rather than badgering. Trust change takes time.

- **Follow through** - Stick to the boundaries you outlined consistently, not just when it's convenient. Act, don't just say.

With patience and compassion on both sides, your family can get to acceptance even if they don't always like or agree with your needed boundaries. Trust that new patterns will emerge.

Rebuilding Broken Trust and Resentments

Long-standing resentments and betrayals of trust within families don't magically disappear. But healing is possible when both parties are willing to understand, empathize, apologize, and reset boundaries.

Here are steps for reconciling when hurt runs deep:

- **Allow emotions to surface** - Suppressing anger or hurt perpetuates dysfunction. Safely exploring these feelings is essential. Consider counseling for mediated discussions.

- **Take ownership** - Begin with "I'm sorry for..." rather than staying on defense. Model vulnerability and accountability without excuses.

- **Share your story** - Explain how the actions impacted you then and to this day. Trauma isn't always visible on the surface. Give context.

- **Listen without interrupting** - Create space for their perspective. Don't get over-focused on rebutting the details. Simply listen and affirm.

- **Identify root insecurities** - What core fears or vulnerabilities underlie behaviors like control or neglect? Seeing below surface helps humanize.

- **Find common ground** - While your experiences differ, look for shared hopes and values like love, trust, honesty, respect, forgiveness.

- **Outline needed changes** - Request specific changes that will rebuild trust and respect for your boundaries moving forward.

- **Forgive, not forget** - You can forgive past harm without naive trust. Use wisdom developed through hardship to reset the relationship on healthier terms.

- **Give it time and space** - Healing doesn't happen instantly after one talk. Allow the process to unfold gradually. Ups and downs are normal.

As long as both parties stay committed to the relationship and growth, great progress can happen. But it does take time, reflection, and perseverance through setbacks.

Strategies for Detaching from Family Dysfunction

In some cases, family dynamics are so dysfunctional that boundaries alone are insufficient. Situations like:

- Repeated abuse or violations of trust
- Active addiction with a reluctance to pursue sobriety
- Serious untreated mental illness that creates chaos
- Ongoing narcissistic behaviors or entitlement
- Extremely controlling or authoritarian parenting

In these cases, creating space or detaching from the family relationship entirely for a period of time (or permanently) may be necessary to protect your well-being.

Here are some strategies:

- **Seek counseling support** - Work with a therapist to process the harms done and strategize next steps. Having an objective professional's input is invaluable.

- **Set clear expectations** - Explicitly outline the behaviors that must change for reconciliation and what actions you'll take if not met.

- **Limit or cease contact** - Based on the severity of issues, restrict or cut off contact for a defined period of time. Or only interact in carefully controlled circumstances like counseling sessions.

- **Disengage from drama** - Opt out of getting embroiled in ongoing chaos. Limit information given to you that may trigger engagement.

- **Surround yourself with healthy people** - Lean on positive friendships that affirm your value. Don't isolate. It's important to see what healthy relationships look like.

- **Practice mindfulness** - Notice when you're ruminating on family troubles. Self-care activities like journaling, exercise, time in nature can help clear your head.

- **Forgive yourself** - Accept that you alone cannot force change. Detaching out of self-protection is not equivalent to abandoning the relationship.

- **Seek support groups** - Join groups like Al-Anon that offer community for dealing with dysfunctional family dynamics. Knowing you're not alone helps.

- **Allow grief** - The loss of family, even a harmful relationship, is painful. Acknowledge the grief so you can move forward in a healthy way.

- **Stay consistent** - Once you've defined boundaries or limits, stick to them. Wavering only enables dysfunction to continue.

Remember that removing yourself from an unhealthy situation doesn't make you cold-hearted. On the contrary - it shows tremendous courage and self-love.

Maintaining Boundaries While Still Being Loving

With skillful, compassionate communication, you can absolutely set firm limits while still conveying warmth in family relationships. Don't make the mistake of equating boundaries with abandonment or rejection.

Here are some principles to integrate both:

- **Lead with love** - Start tough conversations by expressing how much they mean to you. This changes the tone from combative to collaborative.

- **Share your "why"** - Explain that you're creating boundaries to improve your health, reduce anxiety, or be fully present - not out of anger. They'll understand.

- **Use "and" not "but"** - "I love AND need space right now" sounds less harsh than "I love you BUT I need space." Subtle but impactful nuance.

- **Be responsive, not reactive** - Pause before reacting during conflicts. Take a day to cool down before thoughtfully communicating your position.

- **Offer alternatives** - If declining a request, suggest other ways to connect that honor your needs - like brief video chats instead of long visits.

- **Double down on appreciation** - Increases in boundaries necessitate increases in expressed gratitude for their importance in your life.

- **Check the motivation** - Are you setting a boundary from love or uncontrolled anger? Cool down before speaking if emotion is running high.

- **Adjust expectations** - Understand that setting adult boundaries will take time to normalize. Consistency and compassion smooth the transition.

When coming from a centered, calm place, you can absolutely set firm limits while also conveying unwavering love. With practice, the approach will begin to feel more natural. You've got this!

Chapter 4: Creating Work-Life Balance and Boundaries

With the always-on expectations of modern work culture, creating boundaries to protect personal time has never been more essential. Without clear limits, work easily creeps into nights, weekends, holidays, and even into retirement.

But just because you *can* now work 24/7 thanks to technology doesn't mean you should. To avoid burnout, you must define work-life boundaries aligned with your priorities and then stick to them.

This chapter explores how to:

- Set boundaries for availability and responsiveness
- Define appropriate work hours based on your lifestyle
- Limit after-hours work and weekend encroachment
- Take full vacations and sick days guilt-free
- Push back on unrealistic workload expectations
- Prioritize the most important tasks
- Institute boundaries on collaboration and meetings
- Create space for focused solo work
- Avoid overcommitting to new projects
- Model sustainable workload and work-life balance for colleagues

The key is remembering that your worth - both as an employee and a human being - is not defined by constant work and availability.

When you take care of your whole self, you ultimately bring more value to your job as well.

Set Boundaries for Availability and Responsiveness

Unless you have an on-call job with defined emergencies, you have the right to disconnect outside of work hours. Make your available hours known.

Here are some tips:

- **Turn off notifications** - Mute non-urgent messaging apps overnight and on weekends. Set an away message on your work email stating when you'll get back to people.

- **Define response time** - Let people know you aim to respond to messages within 24 hours. Anything more urgent can go higher up.

- **Move at your own pace** - Just because you *receive* a message on your time off does not mean you need to *respond*. Stick to business hours.

- **Model the behavior** - Broadcast your own working hours to set social norms. Others will follow your lead.

- **Use airplane mode** - When traveling or on vacation, set your devices to airplane mode for blocks of time so you can fully unplug and relax.

- **Have a cutoff** - Stop checking emails at a set time each day to fully shift your mind into personal time.

When you consistently stick to defined availability windows, colleagues learn to respect your time. But you have to train their expectations through maintaining boundaries.

Define Appropriate Work Hours Based on Your Lifestyle

Rather than defaulting to the traditional 9-5, identify work hours aligned with your chronotype and responsibilities outside the office. Consider options like:

- **Earlier or later hours** - If you're a morning person, start early and end earlier. Night owls may prefer 11am - 7pm.

- **A compressed 4-day workweek** - Ten hour days for four days allows for three day weekends.

- **Regular half days** - Take Friday afternoons off. Or Wednesday mornings to run errands and appointments.

- **Flexible hours** - Have a set window like 8am - 4pm with flex start and end times for doctor visits or handling family needs.

- **80% schedules** - Move to part time hours temporarily or ongoing to accommodate school, family, hobbies.

- **Remote work** - Eliminate the commute and customize hours more flexibly when working from home.

Discuss appropriate hours with your manager rather than making rogue changes. Explain how the schedule allows you to be most productive. Emphasize you'll get all your work done on time - just at shifted hours.

Limit After Hours Work and Weekend Encroachment

Be vigilant about work creep during your personal downtime. Unless you have an explicit agreement for flexibility, keep weekday nights and weekends sacrosanct through these tips:

- **Keep the calendar blocked** - Just like you block time for meetings, block personal time in your calendar too.

- **Turn off work devices** - Pack away laptops, turn off email, and silence notifications during non-work hours. Remove the temptation and triggers.

- **Let calls go to voicemail** - Unless there's a true emergency, don't answer work calls during personal time. Return the call when you're officially working.

- **Batch administrative tasks** - Group emails, expense reports, etc into set worktimes. Don't let these leak into evenings and weekends.

- **Say no to off-hours meetings** - If asked for after hours meetings, recommend alternatives during your normal availability.

- **Establish quiet hours** - Define chunks of time where you are fully unavailable like 6pm - 8am including weekends.

- **Take real breaks** - Use your lunch break to fully recharge, not just work through it. Go for a walk outside rather than eating at your desk.

Protecting your evenings, weekends, and holidays sends the message that you respect work-life separation. Don't let work become your only identity.

Take Full Vacations and Sick Days Guilt-Free

Many employees feel guilty fully disconnecting on vacation. But time off is essential for avoiding burnout and coming back energized with renewed creativity and motivation.

Here's how to completely unplug:

- **Block time off in advance** - Give plenty of notice for multi-day absences so colleagues can plan around it.

- **Actually, take the time** - Use all your earned vacation and sick days per year. You deserve these benefits.

- **Set an away message** - Post an out of office message with dates you're gone and who to contact for anything urgent. Then disable inbox access so you're not tempted to check messages.

- **Fully detach** - Inform colleagues you will be 100% offline on specific dates and unavailable for calls or emails.

- **Avoid work talk** - Instruct colleagues not to contact you about work matters on your vacation. Enjoy quality time off.

- **Actually take a break** - Don't just work from a different location. Do activities unrelated to your job to come back refreshed.

- **Come back gradually** - If possible, build in a couple transition days to ease back into the workload and catch up on email.

Of course, emergencies happen, but aim to truly protect your time off as much as possible. You return motivated and focused when you properly recharge.

Push Back on Unrealistic Workload Expectations

With increased workload demands, you may need to renegotiate tasks and deadlines. Don't let unreasonable expectations go unaddressed.

Here are tips for having the conversation:

- **Track your time** - Quantify how much time and effort your work actually requires each week. Data helps justify needed changes.

- **Describe your priorities** - Explain what critical projects you want to focus on rather than spreading yourself thin across too many.

- **Outline what's feasible** - Given your other responsibilities and priorities, define how much you can reasonably handle in terms of new projects and quick turnarounds.

- **Involve others** - Identify if you can delegate or collaborate to lighten the load. Don't go it alone when you're overloaded.

- **Propose solutions** - Come ready with ideas like shifting deadlines, dropping certain tasks, or dividing work differently.

- **Define required resources** - Make clear if you need additional staff, tools, or budget to achieve goals with excellence.

- **Communicate calmly** - Don't approach from a place of overwhelm, anxiety or accusation. Have realistic solutions ready.

- **Suggest a trial period** - Propose trying defined boundaries like fewer meetings or earlier departures for 2-3 weeks to test it out.

- **Check for understand** - Ensure your manager understands the need for change. Ask how they envision successfully supporting you.

With data, solutions, and empathy for workplace pressures on your side, most bosses will work to create a sustainable workload and honor your much-needed boundaries.

Prioritize the Most Important Tasks

Constantly working in crisis mode leads to burnout over time. To create focus and calm, practice proactive priority management. Strategies include:

- **Follow the 80/20 rule** - Identify and invest your best energy in the 20% of tasks that generate 80% of impact. Avoid getting overwhelmed by fretting over minor details.

- **Tackle tough tasks first** - Do your most intense thinking and important projects early when motivation and energy are highest. Leave busy work for later.

- **Include buffer time** - Build in breaks between back-to-back meetings and pad longer for big projects in case they take more time. Don't overbook yourself.

- **Manage expectations** - Be upfront about what you can deliver by the deadline given your current workload. Don't overpromise outcomes or availability.

- **Block distraction-free time** - Calendar uninterrupted blocks of 2-4 hours for pushing projects forward without losing focus.

- **Set boundaries on less important work** - Politely push back on requests unrelated to your core role and priorities. Say this is not the best use of your time currently.

- **Check emails on a schedule** - Only allow yourself access at set times, not constantly. Don't let reactivity pull you off-track.

With strong prioritization skills, you regain control of your time and are empowered to work on what matters most to you and the business. The hardest part is simply saying no to the less essential tasks.

Institute Boundaries on Collaboration and Meetings

Colleagues asking for input and impromptu meetings easily fragment focused time. Set some boundaries to protect solo work.

- **Close your door/use a headset** - Non-verbals like avoiding eye contact, using headphones or working in private signal when you are unavailable for quick questions or chats.

- **Limit drop-ins** - Kindly request that colleagues schedule a meeting rather than "swinging by" your office for a few minutes. This forces intentionality.

- **Reduce recurring meetings** - For standing meetings, evaluate if they need the same frequency. Can you shift to once per month vs. weekly?

- **Require an agenda** - Mandate that any meeting request includes a clear purpose and agenda so you join only if truly productive use of time.

- **Shorten meetings** - Default to 30- or 45-minute meetings to remain tightly focused. Extend as needed rather than scheduling too long.

- **Leave buffer time** - Block at least 15 minutes between meetings to regroup and avoid back-to-back rushed scheduling.

- **Encourage written communication** - When possible, request a quick email or chat instead of an in-depth meeting. Written exchanges often provide the clarity needed.

Don't underestimate the compound effect of recurring little interruptions and obligations on your days. Protecting your time benefits your colleagues as well by enabling you to give your best effort to shared work.

Create Space for Focused Solo Work

Some tasks require lengthy uninterrupted focus to maintain a state of flow, like:

- Writing in-depth reports
- Coding or developing programs
- Analyzing complex data
- Learning highly technical skills
- Developing strategy presentations
- Doing research and synthesis

Here are some tips to protect space for deep work:

- **wakes early or stay late** - Use off-peak hours with less meetings and interruptions for ultra-focused work.
- **Work through lunch** - Block lunch as dedicated Zeit time when most colleagues are out of office.
- **Use noise-cancelling headphones** - Show you are unavailable even if physically present in a shared workspace.
- **Book private rooms** - Reserve conference rooms or huddle pods during chaos to simulate a closed office.
- **Convert commuting time** - Utilize your commute for learning or writing if you take public transportation.

- **Disable notifications** - Mute non-essential apps that pull your attention while doing focused work.

- **Put up a "busy" indicator** - Cue coworkers not to disturb you when wearing headphones or displaying other common signals.

- **Work from home** - Choose to telecommute for projects requiring minimal interactions and interruptions.

Don't underestimate the collective toll constant context switching takes on creativity and productivity over time. Protecting boundaries creates the invaluable gift of unbroken focus.

Avoid Overcommitting to New Projects

The desire to prove yourself and take on exciting challenges can lead to counterproductive overextension. Before saying yes, scrutinize bandwidth.

Ask yourself:

- Is this in line with my role and current priorities?

- Do I currently have the bandwidth for additional work?

- Does this align with my learning and growth goals?

- Will I have to deprioritize other important work?

- Can any of the work be delegated to utilize others' strengths?

- Is this timeline realistic given my current commitments?

- Does this project warrant going beyond my capacity?

It's best to promise less and do more rather than promising more and delivering less. Shot down scope creep too. Just because an assignment evolves and grows doesn't mean your time commitment must too. Stick to your original agreement by pushing back on added work.

Saying no to great opportunities is difficult. But taking on too much reduces your contributions everywhere as you get spread thin. Be selective and stay focused on producing excellence.

Model Sustainable Workload and Work-Life Balance for Colleagues

You can't expect colleagues and managers to respect boundaries you don't role model. Lead by example when it comes to reasonable workloads and work-life integration.

Ways to influence team norms include:

- **Leave on time** - Make it a habit to wrap up and depart at your designated end of day rather than lingering indefinitely. Others will follow suit.

- **Take real breaks** - Use vacation days, sick time, and parental leave to demonstrate the importance of recharging. Employees are more likely to do the same after seeing leaders role model it.

- **Verbally reinforce priorities** - Regularly talk about the importance of family time, health, hobbies, etc to signal work isn't everything.

- **Manage reasonable deadlines** - Refuse to set unrealistic last-minute turnarounds that require weekends or overtime. Plan adequately.

- **Check out during time off** - When on vacation, disconnect fully. Colleagues will see they also have permission to set an away message and unplug.

- **Avoid sending late night or weekend emails** - Only correspond during work hours yourself so as not to normalize 24/7 availability.

- **Ask about wellbeing** - Demonstrate care for the whole person by regularly asking how colleagues are managing stress and workload.

- **Host social events** - Build camaraderie by organizing occasional team happy hours, outings, or activities not focused on work.

When leaders honor policies and boundaries themselves, they signal organizational values and acceptable norms for others to follow. Even in high intensity workplaces, you can role model sane boundaries. Don't accept the mentality that you must put up with unreasonable expectations and endless work to succeed. Have courage to forge a new path and bring others with you.

Chapter 5: Managing Toxic Relationships and Poor Boundaries

We all likely have or have had people in our lives that leave us feeling drained, insecure, resentful, or constantly on edge. These toxic relationships hijack our emotions and sabotage our health and self-esteem.

You may feel compelled to keep toxic people close out of guilt, enmeshment, hopes of change, or loneliness. But the healthiest act of love is learning to detach from relationships that consistently cause harm. Remove your energy from what depletes you, and redirect it to those who truly nurture and reciprocate care.

This chapter provides guidance on:

- Recognizing signs of a toxic relationship
- Learning to detach and move on from draining people
- Setting boundaries when required to interact with toxic personalities
- Protecting against manipulation or passive aggressive behavior
- Rebuilding broken trust and resetting boundaries after breaches
- Getting support when leaving an abusive relationship
- How to find peace and closure when detachment is healthiest

The first step is always bringing more self-awareness. From there, you can take brave action to honor and protect your highest wellbeing.

Recognizing Signs of a Toxic Relationship

Toxic relationships exhibit recurring emotional, verbal or physical patterns that leave you feeling belittled, manipulated, rejected, disrespected or confused. Over time, they erode self-esteem and well-being.

Here are some common indicators:

- **You feel frequently on edge** - Being around the person triggers constant anxiety, hypervigilance, people pleasing and walking on eggshells.

- **Your needs are dismissed** - Expressing your boundaries, feelings or requests is consistently met with defensiveness, argument, invalidation, or passive aggressiveness.

- **The relationship is one-sided** - Efforts to connect meaningfully go unreciprocated. Your needs come last as theirs dominate.

- **Conversations often escalate into arguments** - Minor disagreements frequently blow up into major battles. Resolution proves impossible.

- **You feel trapped** - A sense of obligation keeps you in the relationship even when your intuition signals you would be happier free from it.

- **Hot and cold behaviors** - The person oscillates between being loving and approval to suddenly unavailable, critical or rejecting, keeping you constantly chasing emotional connection.

- **Past harms go unresolved** - Patterns of betrayal, broken promises, hurtful words, lies or other breaches of trust continue despite apologies and chances given.

- **Your self-worth suffers** - Being around the person often leaves you feeling bad about yourself, confused, ashamed, insecure, guilty or emotionally exhausted.

- **You hide the real you** - To keep the peace, you mask aspects of your true self, interests, needs, values and opinions to avoid backlash.

- **Depression or anxiety worsens** - The relationship may aggravate mental health conditions leaving you with lowered motivation, loss of joy, or ruminating worries.

Remember - a healthy relationship expands, enriches, and brings out your best self. It does not consistently drain you or require you to shrink, mask, or contort yourself just to prevent fallout. Pay attention when self-neglect starts feeling normal.

Learning to Detach and Move On from Draining People

Ending or limiting contact with toxic people you once cared for brings painful complexity. You may grieve the loss of perceived intimacy or support. But protecting your mental health requires reducing or eliminating harmful connections.

Here are some tips:

- **Gain distance and perspective** - Creating physical and emotional space helps you see just how much the relationship costs your well-being.

- **Sit with your sadness** - Acknowledge grief and other difficult feelings rather than suppressing them. Processing prevents bouncing back to the person out of loneliness.

- **Block their access** - Limit their ability to manipulate or guilt you by blocking their number, email, social media, etc. Sever digital ties.

- **Avoid explaining yourself** - You don't need endless justification to end an unhealthy relationship. State your choice simply without self-blame.

- **Find healthy connections** - Invest time in relationships that make you feel good about yourself, understood and seen. Don't isolate.

- **Release fantasies of change** - Accept the likelihood this person will not change. Focus on your own growth rather than trying to "fix" them.

- **Forgive yourself** - Have compassion for why you may have accepted poor treatment, like past trauma or toxicity modeling. But now do better.

- **Seek counseling** - Work with a therapist skilled at detachment to process grief, gain clarity, and develop healthier relationship skills and self-worth.

The more you engage in caring for and loving yourself, the less you will settle for those who don't value you. You instruct others how to treat you by what you allow.

Setting Boundaries When Required to Interact with Toxic Personalities

Some toxic relationships are unavoidable, like with family members, school peers or coworkers. Reduce harm by setting strict boundaries for engagement.

Keep interactions brief and superficial - Discuss only benign topics briefly when required to interact. Don't get sucked into excessive openness or vulnerability.

- **Avoid one-on-one time** - Only meet in groups to limit exposure. Group settings curb negative behaviors.

- **Limit alcohol** - Beware loosening boundaries under the influence. Avoid excessive drinking around damaging people.

- **Have an exit plan** - Drive separately and keep your departure time flexible in case you need to suddenly leave a bad situation.

- **Ask for space directly** - If conversations turn unhealthy, say explicitly you need to walk away and will reconnect later in a calmer mindset.

- **Don't justify your choices** - Your life decisions are not up for debate or criticism. Decline discussions about boundaries you set.

- **Use physical distance** - Position yourself across the room or table to discourage intimidation or unwelcome touch.

- **Find neutral companions** - Invite someone compassionate as a buffer to toxic events to avoid one-on-one ambush.

- **Keep personal details private** - Share very selectively to avoid manipulation or attempts at unwanted "advice."

The less toxic personalities know about you and your inner world, the less they have to use against you. Keep it surface level, trust your gut, and don't doubt yourself.

Protecting Against Manipulation or Passive Aggressive Behaviors

Toxic relationships often involve manipulative games to gain power and control. But you can neutralize these ploys by recognizing them. Watch for:

- **Guilt trips** - Making exaggerated displays of disappointment to shame you into doing what they want. "I realize you're not genuinely concerned about me."

- **Victim act** - Diverting blame for their harmful actions by playing victim. "I can't fathom that you'd make such a terrible accusation against me."

- **Silent treatment** - Punishing with cold withdrawal if they don't get their way. May use the silent treatment for weeks or months to increase your anxiety.

- **Vaguebooking** - Being purposely ambiguous in social media posts fishing for attention or sympathy. For example: "Can't believe this happened to me. So devastated right now."

- **Triangulation** - Turning other people against you to damage credibility or relationships. Starting false rumors and gossip.

- **Hoovering** - Pretending the relationship is mended after conflicts by being extra nice, caring and attentive to suck you back in before returning to old habits.

- **Gaslighting** - Denying their own mean behaviors while making you question your own sanity and memory. "You're too sensitive. That never happened."

- **Intermittent reinforcement** - Providing affection, approval or support randomly and unpredictably to increase attachment and loyalty. The inconsistency keeps you hooked.

- **Public embarrassment** - Making cutting remarks in front of others to trigger shame. But then passing it off as a joke when confronted.

Don't buy into manipulative pretenses. Name these behaviors directly when you see them. If the toxicity persists, know you have every right to walk away. You deserve so much better.

Rebuilding Broken Trust and Resetting Boundaries After Breaches

We all make relationship missteps needing grace and a second chance. But repeated boundary violations must be addressed for repair and safety. Don't just keep forgiving endlessly.

Steps to rebuild trust include:

- **Make amends** - The offending person takes responsibility through apology and engages in good faith efforts to earn back trust like counseling. Empty apologies breed resent.

- **Share your story** - Explain how the behaviors impacted you without accusing. Providing your context prevents quick minimization.

- **Define needed changes** - Outline explicit changes and new boundaries required to continue the relationship. Don't leave things vague.

- **Enact consequences** - If changes don't occur after a defined timeframe, enact pre-agreed upon consequences like reduced contact. Follow through consistently, not just threats.

- **Reset expectations** - Clarify that previous levels of openness and vulnerability are being scaled back and need to be re-earned over time through consistent positive actions.

- **Assume gradual progress** - Increase contact slowly as trust rebuilds rather than immediately reverting to old habits. Small steps prevent big regressions.

- **Seek counseling** - Work with a counselor to process betrayal and develop skills for setting boundaries, repair conversations, and reducing codependency behaviors.

- **Trust slowly** - Notice when actions consistently match words over an extended time before letting your guard down fully. Don't get lured by short term niceness.

- **Release the need to understand** - Don't obsess over explaining why they acted hurtfully. Just focus on whether real change is happening.

Major trust violations can't be papered over easily. But with effort on both sides, relationships can heal. If no real change results, though, know your limits and when to walk away.

Getting Support When Leaving an Abusive Relationship

In more severe cases of unhealthy relationships marked by abusive behavior, violence, or serious manipulation from an intimate partner, it's essential to carefully plan how to leave the situation safely. Don't stay just hoping they'll change. Seek outside help.

Options include:

- **Calling a domestic violence hotline** - Talk through your situation with someone experienced helping abuse victims leave safely. They can connect you to legal and support resources in your area.

- **Making an exit plan** - Work with counselors to create a detailed plan for leaving that covers housing, financial independence, childcare, legal actions, belongings, schedule logistics and more. Improvising under stress is difficult, so plan ahead.

- **Filing a restraining order** - Involve the police to get legal protection from force, harassment, intimidation or approaching you and your home if you feel in danger.

- **Securing abuse-proof devices** - Get spare cell phones or devices not trackable by the abuser so you can safely make plans and get help. Delete browsing histories.

- **Having an emergency relocation** - Make arrangements ahead of time to stay with trusted friends or family or at a shelter in case you need to leave immediately for safety.

- **Obtaining counseling** - Work with a therapist trained in abuse trauma both during and after the relationship for coping skills, releasing guilt and rebuilding self-worth.

- **Building a support network** - Lean on friends, family, churches, or support groups. You don't have to manage alone. And never stay just because you feel isolated.

Escape is possible with careful strategy and help. Your wellbeing and right to live free of abuse come first. Prioritize safety, counseling and starting the healing process.

How to Find Peace and Closure When Detachment is Healthiest

Letting go of toxic relationships, even when necessary, often brings overwhelming and conflicting emotions. Find peace through self-care and inner wisdom.

- **Release fantasies of change** - Accept that this person is unlikely to transform into who you need them to be. Appreciate actions over intentions or empty promises.

- **Forgive yourself** - Have compassion that you accepted poor treatment, likely resulting from past wounds or unconscious modeling. But now you know better.

- **Invest in present joy** - Focus on relationships and activities that make you feel cared for, alive, and like your best self today. Don't dwell on the past losses.

- **Own your worth** - Remind yourself that removing unhealthy connections reflects deserved self-love. You're teaching others how you want to be treated.

- **Allow processing time** - Be patient through the stages of grief. Feel all the emotions, even the unpleasant ones, so they can move through you.

- **Limit numbing behaviors** - Avoid excessive alcohol, shopping, eating, sleeping, etc just to temporarily check out. Stay present through the pain.

- **Write a goodbye letter** - Express everything you need to - hurt, disappointment, well wishes - in a letter you don't send. Ritualize closure.

- **Celebrate your growth** - Focus on how much stronger and wiser you now are. Let go of victim stories by seeing the gifts in your journey.

- **Look forward** - Spend mental energy envisioning your healthier, happier relationships and life without this person rather than ruminating on the past.

With self-compassion and commitment to your peace, you can process the loss and start your next positive chapter. You've got this!

Chapter 6: Communicating Your Needs Kindly But Firmly

Knowing your boundaries internally is only the first step. The rubber meets the road when expressing them outwardly. Assertive but compassionate communication is key for acceptance.

This chapter provides guidance on:

- Planning boundary conversations proactively
- Using "I" statements to own your experience
- Being specific in your requests
- Softening the delivery without weakening the message
- Responding to defensiveness and pushback
- Setting consequences for boundary violations
- Having boundaries conversations in writing
- Using repetition and consistency to strengthen boundaries
- Setting boundaries while still being kind
- Building confidence through self-affirmations

Let's explore how to articulate your boundaries in a way people can truly hear and understand.

Planning Boundary Conversations Proactively

Delivering firm boundaries effectively involves forethought and strategy. Don't reactively blurt them out in a confrontational manner. Plan the discussion proactively for maximal understanding.

Pick the right time - Choose a time of calm rather than escalation. Don't deliver boundaries in the heat of conflict. Wait for tensions to settle.

Set the scene - Have the conversation privately rather than being overheard. Turn off distractions and make eye contact to convey care.

Know your key needs - Reflect beforehand on your top 1-3 non-negotiable needs you want to communicate. Don't dump a whole laundry list.

Phrase as invitation - "I'd appreciate the opportunity to share some needs and discuss solutions." Frame the chat as a collaborative discussion, not one-way lecturing.

Make requests, not demands - Polite requests are received better than aggressive demands. "I'd appreciate if we could agree on quiet hours after 9pm when you visit."

Have potential compromises in mind - If they push back on a need, propose alternatives that still work for you. Creative problem-solving prevents deadlock.

Ask for their perspective - Learn why they think or behave as they do. See if you can address root causes together through boundary setting.

Suggest a trial run - Pitch your boundaries as an experiment for a defined period. Lower stakes help others feel less defensive.

Thoughtful set up dramatically improves boundary acceptance. Invest time to prepare mentally before difficult conversations.

Using "I" Statements to Own Your Experience

"I" statements are powerful for expressing boundaries non-accusatorily. They focus on owning your own experience and needs rather than blaming the other person.

Some examples:

"I need more notice before visits to keep my anxiety low."

"I don't have the bandwidth to take on more volunteer hours now."

"I feel most loved and cared for when you help with chores without asking."

"I get completely drained after more than 2 hours of social time."

"I feel hurt when my opinion is mocked during family debates."

"I value you immensely AND I also need more alone time."

The "and" in "I love you and..." statements also softens boundaries by affirming the relationship before asserting needs.

Always focus on your realities, feelings and requests rather than criticizing the other person's behavior or character. This reduces their defensiveness.

Being Specific in Your Requests

Vague or passive aggressive boundaries breed confusion and non-compliance. Always be clear, direct and specific in defining your needs.

Specify:

- Exact behaviors you want added or avoided
- Timeframes or frequencies that work for you
- The impact on your thoughts, feelings or health
- Appreciation for their efforts in advance

Rather than "I need you to be more considerate when you come over," say "I'd really appreciate if you could give me 3-4 days notice before visits and avoid showing up after 9pm. The surprise stresses me out."

The more details you provide, the higher the likelihood your needs will be understood and honored. Don't beat around the bush or expect them to read your mind.

Softening the Delivery Without Weakening the Message

You can set firm boundaries while still being gentle and compassionate in your delivery. The tone and manner of your expression matter more than the actual words you use.

Strategies include:

- **Leading with affection or appreciation** - Start the conversation by expressing care and importance of the relationship before discussing the issue. This primes them to be less defensive.

- **Watching your tone and body language** - Speak calmly without raising your voice. Maintain open relaxed posture. This communicates your boundaries aren't an attack but coming from care.

- **Making eye contact** - Looking someone in the eyes says you see them and the relationship matters. Avoiding eye contact conveys detachment.

- **Allowing pauses after the request** - Give them a moment to process before immediately requiring an answer. More time to absorb prevents quick knee-jerk rejection.

- **Asking for their perspective** - Inquire about their take on the situation and if they have any needs to share too. Creating a two-way dialogue prevents power struggles.

- **Suggesting compromises** - Offer middle ground solutions that respect their needs too. Collaboration has mutual buy-in.

Healthy boundaries should leave both people feeling heard, loved, and secure - not defeated. Soften without weakening your core message.

Responding to Defensiveness and Pushback

No matter how tactful you are, some people will still respond to boundaries with resistance or dismissal. Don't let it discourage you. Manage it calmly.

If they get defensive or undermining, try:

- **Hearing them out** - Let them fully share their reaction without interrupting them. Feel understood first before restating your needs.

- **Reframing positively** - "I know this is an adjustment, but I'm hopeful we can make it work over time." Put a solutions-focused spin.

- **Compassionately acknowledging their view** - "I appreciate you see it that way. My perspective is..." or "I know my request challenges norms/expectations..."

- **Looping back to the core need** - "Ultimately the reason I'm asking for this is so I can have energy left at the end of the day for us."

- **Providing choices** - "Which of these options feels most workable for you?" Offering options enables everyone to feel acknowledged while also maintaining boundaries.

- **Suggesting a trial run** - "Why don't we try this for a couple weeks and see how it goes?" A test phase feels lower stakes.

Stay centered in your right to healthy boundaries. Don't escalate or get derailed into tangents. Stick clearly to your needs and remember this will get easier with practice.

Setting Consequences for Boundary Violations

Consistently upholding your stated boundaries is crucial. Don't let violations slide just to keep the peace. Follow up with natural consequences.

If I say my child cannot have screen time after 8pm but notice it happening anyway, an appropriate consequence is to take away devices at that bedtime. The result directly correlates.

Other examples:

- If a friend is routinely very late, the consequence is leaving if they don't arrive by a defined time.

- If a coworker ignores your request not to disturb you during focus hours, the consequence is forwarding their emails/calls to someone else until your requested time is up.

- If family constantly presses you for details about your dating life against your wishes, the consequence is cutting visits short.

- If a partner forgets to support agreed upon chores, the consequence is ordering takeout rather than cooking dinner together.

- If a roommate disregards your quiet hours request, the consequence is investing in noise cancelling headphones to block it out.

The consequence should match the action, not escalate it. The goal is upholding your boundary, not punishment. Make sure you follow through consistently, not just threaten.

Having Boundaries Conversations in Writing

Sensitive or complex conversations are sometimes easier in writing. You can carefully edit your words and provide nuanced explanations.

Tips for writing effective boundary emails/texts:

- **Strike a kind but serious tone** - Pleasant but firm. Make clear you expect follow through.

- **Provide background and context** - Share when the issue arose, how it makes you feel, impacts on you etc.

- **Be specific in requests** - Don't leave actions open to interpretation. Give precise behavioral steps.

- **Suggest a phone/in-person discussion** - Offer to chat more. Communication mediums each have pros and cons. Use judiciously.

- **Express your flexibility** - Ask how you might both compromise to resolve the issue together.

- **Affirm the relationship** - Close by conveying appreciation and hope for mutual understanding.

- **Allow time for processing** - Wait to approach in-person after they've had time to absorb your email. Don't require an instant reaction.

Written communication works best for reasonable people willing to see your perspective. It likely won't penetrate toxic resistance. Know your audience.

Using Repetition and Consistency to Strengthen Boundaries

One polite conversation will rarely alter lifelong habits or dysfunctional patterns. Expect to repeat your boundaries frequently. Consistency matters most.

Ways to drive boundaries home:

- **Communicate on multiple channels** - For example, say it verbally but also text it so they can re-read and absorb it better.

- **Don't assume one talk tackles it** - Follow up if old behaviors start creeping back in. Changing habits takes reminding.

- **Keep language consistent** - Stick to the same phrases, standards and consequences. Consistent words drill it in.

- **Praise progress** - If steps are taken in the right direction, express appreciation. Positive reinforcement!

- **Progress over perfection** - Allow leeway and growing pains as they learn new ways of relating. But don't drop boundaries.

- **Refer back to past talks** - "As we discussed last month, I need at least 24 hours notice before a visit." Shows it's not a one-off plea.

- **Put it in writing** - Send a quick email or text recapping your boundary as a reference. Written records are powerful.

- **Stay calm but serious** - Don't get exasperated they "don't get it." Keep your tone neutral and briefly reiterate needs if they "forget."

Give people grace as they adjust but stay resolved. Consistency demonstrates you mean what you say.

Setting Boundaries While Still Being Kind

Some people incorrectly associate boundaries with aggression, attack, or meanness. But quite the opposite is true. Healthy boundaries allow kindness - towards yourself and others.

You can be both compassionate and direct by:

- **Speaking calmly and respectfully** - Blurting needs harshly in the heat of anger just fuels defensiveness. Keep cool.

- **Affirming the relationship** - Assure the person they matter to you before diving into issues. This changes the tone.

- **Listening to their side** - Ask why they do the problematic behavior or feel hurt by the boundary. Seek understanding.

- **Expressing appreciation** for past and current efforts, even if incomplete. Giving credit builds goodwill and motivation.

- **Allowing time to process** - Don't demand an immediate reaction. Give space for high emotions to settle before re-addressing later.

- **Leading with empathy** for their objections or struggles with the boundary. "I know this transition is tough. I am really grateful that you've listened to me."

- **Compromising when possible** - If a need isn't non-negotiable, offer flexibility so it's not your way or the highway.

- **Being positive** - Compliment behaviors aligning with your boundary. Encourage baby step progress rather than harping on slip-ups.

Boundaries aren't about dictating your demands. They are about calmly creating mutually healthy relationships - starting with your relationship with yourself.

Building Confidence Through Self-Affirmations

Old habits of people pleasing and prioritizing others die hard.

Combat engrained doubt by building self-trust.

Try writing empowering affirmations about your right to boundaries.

For example:

"I deserve to feel safe, comfortable, and respected at all times."

"My needs and feelings matter."

" I'm showing courage by expressing myself, even if it feels uncomfortable."

"I can handle others' initial anger or disappointment about boundaries."

"If the relationship is harmed by me honoring my needs, it wasn't healthy to begin with."

"I teach others how I want to be treated by what I accept from them."

" I opt for well-defined limits driven by self-care, not self-centeredness."

Repeat supportive mantras daily until they feel true in your core. Don't let self-doubt sabotage the positive growth you're making. What other affirmations would boost your confidence in maintaining boundaries? Write them out. Self-encouragement trains your mind to become your ally, not critic. You've got this!

Chapter 7: Overcoming Guilt, Anxiety, and Pushback

Even when you know intellectually you deserve boundaries, emotionally you may still struggle. Guilt, people-pleasing habits, anxiety about others' reactions, and assuming responsibility for other's feelings die hard.

But with practice building self-confidence and recognizing unhealthy messaging, you can overcome self-doubt and stick to your boundaries with calm resolve.

This chapter explores strategies to manage:

- Letting go of guilt and obligation
- Coping with disapproval or anger from others
- Responding to accusations of being "selfish"
- Overcoming anxiety about being viewed negatively
- Defining your role versus taking undue responsibility
- Maintaining boundaries gently but firmly
- Creating physical and emotional space when needed
- Developing a supportive community
- Working through past trauma that affects boundaries
- Being kind toward yourself throughout the journey

As we build the skills to define boundaries and honor them with compassionate courage, we transform not just our relationships, but how we feel about ourselves.

Letting Go of Guilt and Obligation

After a lifetime of putting others first, guilt often arises when establishing new boundaries. You may worry:

- I'm letting people down

- It's my job to make them happy

- I'm acting selfish

- I ought to be capable of managing greater challenges.

But these messages reflect engrained habits, not truth. Establishing sound boundaries is not self centered - they are self-care. Feelings of obligation mean you've overextended.

Here are some ways to release misplaced guilt:

- **Question the messages** - Ask yourself: *"Would I judge someone else harshly for setting this boundary? Or just myself?"* Consider what advice you would give a friend.

- **Accept that guilt is part of change** - Making significant life changes of any kind naturally brings up guilt and remorse over leaving the old way or disappointing people. Expect the feelings, but don't let them derail progress.

- **Refocus on your needs** - Guilt redirects attention to how choices affect others. Refocus on how the boundary benefits your health and wellbeing.

- **Let others manage themselves** - You are not responsible for others' feelings or how they "cope" with your boundaries. They are capable of regulating their own emotions.

- **Talk it through** - Discuss guilt openly with supportive friends. Verbalizing shame often lessens its power. Hear you are not alone.

- **Practice self-compassion** - Be kind to yourself as you learn new emotional habits. Change takes time. Celebrate each small act of self-care.

- **Make time for joy** - When you notice guilt creeping in, intentionally shift your thoughts to something that lights you up.

Guilt may never fully disappear, but you don't need to let it run you either. Expect guilt but act "as if" - as if deserving healthy boundaries is your new normal.

Coping With Disapproval or Anger From Others

Even when you communicate boundaries gently and diplomatically, some people respond with disapproval, resistance, or even anger. This might include:

- Passive aggressive comments
- Direct accusations of being "selfish," "difficult," or "oversensitive"
- Mockery of your needs and restating their opposing views
- Over-the-top emotional displays designed to make you feel guilty
- Veiled threats about ending the relationship or cutting you off

Their reactions likely stem from perceived loss of control or fear of change more so than actual harm caused by the boundary itself. Don't let their emotions derail your self-care.

Here are some tips for managing pushback:

- **Hear them out** - Let them fully vent and get their grievances off their chest without arguing back.

- **Empathize** - "I understand this is disappointing. Please know I still care deeply about you and our relationship."

- **Reaffirm the need** - Restate plainly what you require moving forward and why it's important for your wellbeing.

- **Give reassurance** - If they fear losing you, emphasize you are just improving the relationship, not abandoning it.

- **Don't apologize or back down** - Kindly but firmly stick to your guns. Their overreactions do not invalidate your needs.

- **Give space** - If emotions escalate, call a break in the conversation. Let everyone cool off before revisiting.

- **Set consequences** - Inform them if disrespect continues, you'll politely remove yourself until they can discuss calmly. And follow through.

Stay confident in the face of temper tantrums, guilt trips, manipulation, or other fear-based tactics. You are not responsible for their feelings. Nor does their discomfort justify revoking your own care.

Responding to Accusations of Being "Selfish"

One of the most common accusations when establishing boundaries is that you're being "selfish." This criticism often stings because it triggers our own engrained self-shaming.

If called selfish, try responding:

"I'm making a conscious decision to prioritize self-care over self-neglect". It's about recognizing that I need to take care of myself first in order to be in a position to care for others, especially after a lifetime of feeling drained.

"Taking care of my well-being enables me to be completely available for others." - When you give while running on empty, you often become irritable and impatient.

"I wish caring for myself didn't feel so uncomfortable." - It can help to express empathy that this shift challenges old habits of self-sacrifice you're mutually accustomed to. But you need it.

"My wellbeing matters too." - There are gentle ways to set limits that allow both people's needs to be met. It's not either-or. But you are worthy of care too.

"I'm doing this from a place of love, not selfishness." When boundaries come from self-love and desire for health, they cultivate better relationships, not harm them.

Remember - you cannot pour from an empty cup. Treating yourself with the care, protection, and respect you deserve allows you to act from abundance, not scarcity. That is beautiful self care, not selfishness.

Overcoming Anxiety About Being Viewed Negatively

Early on especially, setting boundaries often brings up fears about how you'll be perceived. Worries might include:

- They'll think I'm selfish
- They'll be angry
- They'll judge me as "difficult"
- They'll see me as cold or unloving
- It will irreparably damage our relationship
- I'll end up abandoned and alone

But research shows these anxieties about being viewed negatively are exaggerated in our heads. If boundaries communicate lovingly, most reasonable people respond with understanding, even when disappointed. Their displeasure is temporary. But when you honor your needs, you build emotional maturity and self-esteem that lasts forever.

Here are some ways to overcome anxiety about others' reactions:

- **Remember that discomfort is temporary** - The awkwardness of change subsides as the new patterns become normal. Don't let short term fears stop you.

- **Ask yourself, "What if...?"** - Consider the most adverse outcome and evaluate if you could manage it. Frequently, we can, even if it's a bit uncomfortable.

- **Focus on how you'll feel with better boundaries** - Anxiety tells you to focus how others might feel about your changes. But shift the focus back to the benefits for *your* health and happiness. That is what matters.

- **Visualize possible reactions** - Envision how they might respond reasonably and unreasonably. Knowing what to expect prevents being blindsided.

- **Practice self-soothing** - When worries creep up, relax through exercises like deep breathing, meditation, soothing music, or cuddling a pet. Activities that calm your nervous system short-circuit anxiety loops.

- **Share your feelings with safe friends** - They can talk you through worries and provide reassurance that you aren't "crazy" for feeling nervous.

Anxiety never fully disappears. But each time you push through it builds your confidence that the worst-case scenario is usually not what happens, and even if it did, you would manage. You've got this!

Defining Your Role vs Taking Undue Responsibility

Without boundaries, we easily take on undue responsibility for other's choices, emotions, and inability to cope healthily with life stressors. Their problems quickly become our problems.

Here are some ways to define your role in relationships more clearly so you don't take on burdens beyond your control:

- **Clarify your responsibilities** - Which people and outcomes can you reasonably hold yourself accountable for? For example, you are responsible for your kids' safety, but not their inner happiness.

- **Accept what you can and can't change** - Serenity prayer wisdom: Focus your energy where you have influence, and leave the rest to the universe. Limit worrying over uncontrollable things.

- **Allow natural consequences** - If you shield someone from the outcomes of their decisions, they don't develop resilience and accountability. Let them experience the results.

- **Offer support, not solutions** - Empathize without trying to fix their problems. RESCUERS become ENABLERS.

- **Manage your reactions** - You can't control others' choices but you can control how much time and energy you expend being upset by them. Focus forward.

- **Set limits around emotional dumping** - It's ok to say "I don't have capacity for venting today, but I'm always here to help problem solve solutions together."

- **Don't assume worst case scenarios** - Getting caught up in their catastrophic thinking pulls you off balance. Don't wildly extrapolate. Deal with what is.

- **Suggest counseling support** - For ongoing issues professionally above your pay grade, gently guide them to get the expert help they need while setting limits around what you can provide.

Stay grounded in your lane. You are never responsible for making choices for others or fixing situations beyond your control. Maintain boundaries around emotional dumping, worry, and problem saturation.

Maintaining Boundaries Gently But Firmly

Equally important as setting boundaries is maintaining them long term, even when uncomfortable. Consistency builds trust in the changes.

Tips for gentle but firm follow-through:

- **Start small** - Tackle minor boundary issues first before moving to more ingrained patterns. Small wins build confidence.

- **Respond, don't react** - If your boundaries are tested, pause mentally first before responding. Don't counterattack. Stay neutral.

- **Use a mantra** - Have a simple phrase like "This is important for my health" that keeps you centered in turbulence.

- **Know it gets easier** - Like building any muscle, saying no and upholding boundaries strengthens with practice. Persist through wobbles.

- **Remind people as needed** - If old patterns re-emerge, restate your boundary kindly and clearly. Say you want to honor new agreements.

- **Stay calm** - Breathe consciously. Don't get baited into heated arguments. Cool heads prevail.

- **Don't justify** - Arguments invite you to defend yourself. But you don't owe endless explanations for healthy boundaries.

- **Give reassurance** - Affirm if others fear your boundaries mean you don't care. For example, tell family your rules ultimately nurture your relationship so you can keep being close as adults. But you need some shifts to make that work long term.

- **Enact consequences** - If someone continues to cross stated boundaries, enact proportional, logical consequences. Maintain them until the boundary is respected.

You can be both compassionate and firm in upholding boundaries. With time, your new communication patterns will feel natural to you - and those around you.

Creating Physical and Emotional Space When Needed

In some instances, managing others' reactions may require temporarily limiting contact to allow emotions to settle. Especially when repeatedly provoked, creating space is wise.

Here are some tips:

- **No ultimatums** - Avoid threatening to cut off contact just to get them to change. Ultimatums often backfire long-term once the control stops.

- **Limit time together** - If visits or events become emotionally charged, gradually reduce how long you spend around certain people. Brief doses are more manageable.

- **Cordially decline invitations** - Politely say no to events you are not required to attend if you need space from someone creating stress.

- **Screen calls** - Let calls go to voicemail from those who drain you so you can prepare mentally before engaging. Or communicate mainly through email/text if it allows you to stay calmer.

- **Disable notifications** - Mute text/email notifications from emotionally triggering people so you aren't alerted every time they contact you. Check on your own terms.

- **Take well-being breaks** - When interactions become toxic, directly but politely state you need to pause contact for a set period to focus on your mental health. Then do it.

- **Surround yourself with positivity** - Lean on relationships that make you feel cared for, energized, and hopeful when needing a reset. Don't isolate yourself.

With toxic relationships, space is often the only way to gain enough separation to detect and reset unhealthy patterns. Protect your peace of mind.

Developing a Supportive Community

Don't underestimate the power of a strong support network as you establish new boundaries. Trying to go it alone makes change much harder. Enlist your "team".

Great support sources include:

- **Counselors** - Therapists provide professional guidance tailored to your situation and struggles with boundary setting.

- **Close friends/family** - Share your journey with a few trusted supporters who will cheer you on. Ask them to check in on your progress and not let you slide backward.

- **Support groups** - Whether in-person or online, groups for issues like codependency, narcissistic abuse, etc offer solidarity and proven advice.

- **Classes/books** - Growth through workshops, self-help books, etc gives you new skills and perspective. Avoid trying to just willpower your way through.

- **Discussion forums** - Anonymous forums allow you to share challenges and get feedback from objective strangers in the same boat.

- **Boundaries role models** - Spend time with people who have healthy boundaries you admire. Let them inspire you through their example.

- **Self-care** - Carve out time for restorative activities like yoga, hiking, massage, art etc to manage stress. Don't burn out.

You don't have to navigate this alone. Ask for help and be humble enough to accept it. Boundaries take a village!

Working Through Past Trauma Affecting Boundaries

For some, weak boundaries stem from emotional wounds and past trauma causing:

- Fear of rejection, criticism or abandonment
- Needing approval and external validation
- Difficulty identifying Manipulation or toxicity
- Lack of trust in one's own instincts and judgment

- Persistent negative self-talk and guilt

In these cases, therapy to process painful experiences can help strengthen boundaries long-term.

Some options:

- **Talk therapy** - Cognitive behavioral and dialectal behavioral therapy help challenge limiting beliefs and build self-worth.

- **Inner child work** - Learning to re-parent and comfort your wounded inner child through visualization or role play builds self-acceptance.

- **Shadow work** - Exposing suppressed emotions to bring subconscious patterns into conscious awareness.

- **EMDR** - Eye movement desensitization and reprocessing to remove trauma blockages.

- **Group sessions** - Shared experiences in group settings provide validation.

- **Self-help books** - Titles dealing with codependency, emotional abuse recovery, assertiveness training etc provide guidance.

- **Mindfulness practices** - Meditation, yoga, spending time in nature help regulate the nervous system.

- **Transition support** - Having an empathetic counselor's ongoing support helps stay strong when facing backlash while transforming old relationship patterns.

Seeing your struggles reflected in others who have overcome them builds faith that you can too. Give yourself patience and compassion as you do the work.

Being Kind to Yourself Throughout the Journey

Learning to set boundaries after a lifetime without them feels monumentally hard. Be gentle with yourself all along the path rather than punishing perceived failures. Progress takes time.

Stay motivated through:

Celebrating small wins - Recognize each tiny step forward like briefly stating a need or spending an hour alone when you used to isolate. Mark progress.

Avoiding comparison - Don't measure your success by anyone else's. We all start from a different place. Meet yourself where you are.

- **Taking breaks** - On exhausting days, give yourself permission to pause the work. Rest and ease up when you hit an emotional wall.

- **Talking through setbacks** - When you slip into old patterns, discuss it with a counselor or supportive friend. Process constructively.

- **Reminding yourself "progress over perfection"** - Embrace good enough efforts, knowing they will build incrementally over time into transformation.

- **Letting go of "should's"** - Don't beat yourself up over what you "should" be able to handle or shaming your needs. Listen within.

- **Doing centering practices** - Develop a mindfulness routine like meditating or walking in nature to calm your nervous system when overwhelmed.

- **Avoiding numbing behaviors** - Be cautious of overusing food, alcohol, shopping etc in response to the discomfort of change. Stay present through the process.

- **Trusting the direction** - Even two steps forward and one step back still trends in the right direction. Expect ups and downs.

Rather than demand instant progress, celebrate your intention and commitment to growth. With compassionate self-care, you will transform. Keep going!

Conclusion

If you've made it to this final chapter, congratulations on investing in your growth and completing this book! I hope you now feel equipped with greater understanding, strategies and courage to start implementing boundaries that transform your life and relationships for the better.

We covered a lot of ground together. Let's recap the key lessons:

Recapping The Main Takeaways

- **Boundaries are essential, not selfish** - Saying no and setting clear limits allows you to protect your time, energy, and emotional availability so you don't end up depleted and overwhelmed. Operating from a state of rest and abundance allows you to then give freely.

- **Know your needs and limits** - Get clear on your own rhythms, values, priorities, dealbreakers, and emotional capacity. Self-knowledge provides the compass to then set boundaries aligned with your truth.

- **Communicate clearly and calmly** - Kind but direct communication gives boundaries the best chance of being understood and respected. Plan conversations ahead of time and practice.

- **Start small** - Don't overhaul everything at once. Build confidence with minor boundaries first before working up to more ingrained patterns. Small steps build momentum.

- **Expect resistance and discomfort** - Even well-intended boundaries can trigger others' defensiveness and make you feel guilty or anxious. Anticipate those emotions, but don't let them derail doing what you know is right. The discomfort passes.

- **Stay consistent** - Consistency builds trust and new habits much more than intensity. Calmly reinforce your boundaries as needed until they become normalized.

- **Surround yourself with support** - Seek supportive friends, family, counselors, and community resources to help motivate and guide you. We all need allies on our path.

- **Keep growing self-awareness** - Re-evaluate your evolving needs periodically. What energizes you and causes resentment may change over time. Update boundaries accordingly. It's a lifelong practice.

Troubleshooting Setbacks

Now you have all the core knowledge and tools needed to transform your relationships and inner peace through healthy boundaries. But change isn't linear. Ups and downs are inevitable. When you stumble, avoid beating yourself up. Reframe setbacks as opportunities to fine-tune your approach. Analyze what went wrong and course correct.

Common roadblocks and how to address them:

- **Feeling Guilty** - Question limiting beliefs about self-care being selfish. Would you judge a friend harshly for needing breaks? Offer yourself the identical kindness and empathy.

- **People-pleasing Habits** - Remind yourself you aren't responsible for others' feelings or how they cope with your boundaries. You have permission to do what feels right for you.

- **Weak Self-Esteem** - Low self-worth often drives over-compliance. Building self-love through therapy, affirmations, and lifestyle choices establishes needed confidence.

- **Not Voicing Needs** - Staying silent builds unhealthy resentment over time. Practice expressing needs calmly. Most people respond well to direct but caring communication.

- **Ambiguous Requests** - Vague pleas get ignored while specific and behavioral asks have more impact. As an illustration: "Kindly refrain from discussing my physical appearance" compared to "Please avoid making comments about what I eat or my body size."

- **Inconsistent Follow-Through** - Sporadic boundaries train people you don't really mean what you say. Stick to defined limits consistently even when it's uncomfortable until the new habits solidify.

- **People Testing Limits** - Restate limits neutrally when tested. For example: "As we agreed, I'm not available for childcare on weekends." Stay unprovoked.

- **Unhealthy Relationships** - You can't coerce toxic people to change through boundaries alone. In those cases, limiting or cutting off contact may be healthiest if attempts to repair fail.

- **Self-Doubt** - Anxiety, guilt, or low confidence may sabotage you. Combat negative self-talk with affirmations, mantras, counseling, and remembering boundaries get easier.

- **Lack of Support** - Having trusted friends and professionals holding you accountable provides needed strength and guidance to stay the course when you feel shaky.

- **Losing Resolution** - Major change takes sustained focus over months and years, not just introductory enthusiasm. When motivation lags, review your core reasons for boundaries and how they'll improve your life.

Imperfect action is always preferable to perfect inaction. You can course-correct along the way. Trust that showing up for yourself leads to positive growth, even if the steps feel shaky at first. Give it time.

Final Encouragement

Reclaiming your life, energy, and schedule for self-care will feel uncomfortable at times but so worth it. Regaining control of your health, time, and mental space cultivates profound benefits:

- Deeper connections based on mutual care and respect
- Greater calm, confidence, and emotional maturity
- Improved concentration and creativity
- Time and energy to invest in your priorities
- More enjoyment of downtime free of guilt and anxiety
- Relief from resentment, bitterness, and burnout
- Increased self-trust and intuition
- A greater feeling of empowerment and freedom

You deserve all of this and more. But only you can take responsibility through setting the boundaries that grant you a peaceful, purposeful, balanced life.

The work at times feels difficult, but the rewards are immense. Stay patient and loving with yourself throughout the journey of growth. You've got this! Here's to living life beautifully on your own terms. Enjoy the liberation!

About the Author

Monday Farouq is an author and licensed psychologist passionate about helping others establish healthy boundaries and balance. After witnessing the toll of poor boundaries and chronic stress in his work, Monday was inspired to write this book sharing his insights and practical strategies for knowing your limits, caring for yourself first, transforming relationships, and ultimately taking charge of your life. Monday hopes to empower readers to gain the confidence and tools to set loving boundaries that protect their peace of mind and nurture mutual understanding. He currently resides in Lagos, Nigeria.